To the people like me
who ride the waves of emotions
Our highs are as high as
the tallest mountain peak
Our lows are as low as the deepest depths
of the ocean.
You are not alone.
There is one who knows everything you feel,
And He still loves you deeply

And to my dad,
Steve Moore
1970–2000

Life so Far

LINDSEY CHRISTIAN

CLAY BRIDGES
PRESS

Life So Far

Published by Clay Bridges Press in Houston, TX
www.ClayBridgesPress.com

ISBN: 978-1-68488-163-5
eISBN: 978-1-68488-164-2

Contents

Chapter 1
Purpose

To begin, to help you understand . . .

Let me show you why I have begun such an endeavor.

Every day, people die
People experience grief
Every day, trees are cut down

Every day, people live on
People experience firsts
Every day, seeds take root

Death
Life
Ends
Beginnings

Over and
Over and
Over it goes

But as a wise woman once taught me,
"Just keep moving forward." —Rosalind

Well, Ms. Roz, this is me moving forward, stepping out into another day yet again. Whether it be storm clouds or sunshine, I choose to either feel the warmth of the sun on my uplifted face or the cool caress of the rain's soothing touch running down my cheeks.

And today, with the sky so clear and blue, with the wind so soft and warm like a heavy blanket wrapped around my shoulders, it feels like the perfect day to sit on the porch with a mug of coffee and tell you my story. In the pages that follow, there will be no defined order; each passage will leap back and forth through time. The only thing they reflect is the way my mind works, flitting from the past to the present and back again.

But I must ask myself, to what end do I tell my story? What is my goal for these pages? Is life the sum of what happens or the wisdom you gain from it? This is not a book about loss, grief, life, love, or the choices we make. It is, in a sense, a testimony of a life lived . . . so far. I present it to you so you know that life is messy, emotions are messy, and my house is often messy too. Take these passages as you will, but know that I don't mean to give guidance; instead, I would like to just be honest. For me, this is what life looks like: a big jumble of every kind of emotion. Come into my mess with me, and I hope it encourages you to let someone into your mess too.

I have some questions that have formed in my mind as I move forward. Perhaps I will understand myself a little better in the end. Through the reading of old journals and seeing trauma after trauma, whether it be self-inflicted or not, I ask myself: Who could really understand? Who could make a determination based on what I tell you? Some would say, with righteous indignation in their tone, that I blame myself. They say, "Has anyone ever told you that it's not your fault?"

But I ask, why do we not take accountability? Certainly, other people's free will comes into play throughout our lives and contributes. However, that does not excuse our own actions; it does not mean we have no accountability. Hear me, this is important. I am not saying that "you are to blame for the things done to you." Absolutely not. I am saying to own yourself and your actions. You also have free will. Do not let the things inflicted upon you become the reasons or justifications for everything that follows.

You have been given the opportunity of life. We do not each exist only in our own simulations but in an intricately woven web of the lives each person on the planet is living. Kaily's actions affect Brittany, and Brittany's reactions affect Jessica, and so on. Brittany cannot control Kaily's actions, but she does have a choice moving forward. She has the choice to look back on a life well lived. She can choose to live in a silo and blame someone else's actions for her own, or she can bloom like a field full of wildflowers blossoming and spreading a vision of joy and peace—an example to Jessica of what life can look like when we stop justifying our actions.

Let's start with a question.

Have you ever known peace? Every day is a choice—a choice to despair at the flat tire, the unexpected migraine, or the rained out ball game. To despair at the dreaded diagnosis or the loss of a job or a friend.

Or it could be an opportunity to choose hope in the face of struggles. It can be a choice to praise God despite our limited view of the future.

SHOUT JOYFULLY TO GOD, ALL THE EARTH! SING ABOUT THE GLORY OF HIS NAME; MAKE HIS PRAISE GLORIOUS. SAY TO GOD, "HOW AWE-INSPIRING ARE YOUR WORKS! YOUR ENEMIES WILL CRINGE BEFORE YOU BECAUSE OF YOUR GREAT STRENGTH. ALL THE EARTH WILL WORSHIP YOU AND SING PRAISE TO YOU. THEY WILL SING PRAISE TO YOUR NAME." SELAH.

—PS. 66:1–4 HCSB

September 2024

Somewhere in Southern Utah

How can I express the beauty of the trees?

Their slender pale branches reach toward the sun. They are like arms lifted in praise.

There is beauty in their pale, smooth skin and their golden crown of leaves, beauty like that of a bride on her wedding day.

They are not greedy with the light of the sun, but they reflect the life they have been given. Generous are they with what they have.

They sing a soft song in the breeze, a hushed whisper of life, joy, and peace.

My Reflection

The calm has been so deceitful in my life. Calmness breeds complacency, and in turn, complacency breeds Pride. "Look and see what I have done." Pride deceives you into thinking Vulnerability is the enemy when, in fact, Pride is stealing away Opportunity. And then suddenly, an opportunity is lost. But was it really sudden?

June 11, 2020

It's just a day at work, and as I stare blankly at my computer. It shifts to a new background, and a verse catches my eye. In that second, a screen pops up and covers some of it so it looks something like this:

Why am I ______________
Why is my ______________
I will put my ________________
I will praise ________________
My savior ______________

It reminded me of my current prayer life. I feel so distant from God, so distracted from Him and his purpose for my life. I feel off-center and so fearful of what the next day will bring. I find it so hard to pray throughout my day, and when I do, it is jumbled and filled with groans for the words I cannot find to express how I feel. It tends to sound a lot like what I saw in my background—just half-finished sentences and lost words. However, today I am reminded that even if the writer could not find the words to complete the verse of this psalm, God knows.

Why am I discouraged?
Why is my heart so sad?
I will put my hope in God!
I will praise Him again—
My Savior and my God!
—Ps. 42:11 NLT

My Reflection

Sometimes all this reflection leaves me baffled. One day I can be so led by faith and encouraged through Scripture, and the next I am led entirely by emotions, feeling too much, and then not enough. I am on a constant quest for balance that never seems to come. Where is the balance between faith and emotions?

October 1, 2024

At the coffee shop, I stare at the blank paper, thinking of all the times I have stared at it before.

How does a person convey the depths of their feelings when they don't know what they feel?

When all the emotions are on top of each other to the point that you do not know if you are feeling everything or nothing . . .

Is there really a difference?

My Reflection

This is my prayer for you:

I pray that you are filled with love and joy and peace.

I pray that your heart is not sad or discouraged.

I pray that with hope, you will lift your face to the heavens.

Cry out to God.

Share with Him your burdens and sorrows.

Empty your heart at His feet.

I pray you know where your hope comes from.

I pray blessings on you and your family.

I pray for wisdom for you and those who come after you.

God, heal their broken hearts.

Draw them in to You.

Give shelter from the storm.

I pray that you know God's love, a love far more than anything we could think to comprehend.

I pray that in the darkest hours, you cry out to Him.

He will hear your cry.

Give them peace of mind knowing You are in control.

I pray you run to Him with arms wide open.

I pray you give your burdens to Him, your hope for salvation.

I pray you know that you have never been alone.

You have never been alone.

You are God's creation; He longs for you. Yes, *you*! Even with the sin you want to hide. Even with the choices you have made that you want to believe are okay. Because you say, "He loves me," that is your justification. Yes! He does love you; you are His beloved, but He hates sin! Cast it out from your life and return to Him.

I will give them a heart to know Me, that I am Yahweh. They will be My people, and I will be their God because they will return to Me with all their heart.

—Jer. 24:7 HCSB

September 30, 2013

Sometimes in life a person can get into a hole so deep that circumstances seem unchangeable. They feel nasty from the dirt caving in over them, and the stains are so hard to hide. Life can reach a point where it no longer seems worth living.

I pondered how to stop thinking, but it was so hard. Maybe if I listened more? It did not work; it was as if I could not even hear because my thoughts were so loud. How can I make them stop? "I am not going to stop thinking 'til I die. Die, die, that's it. I have to die! How does someone die without causing much pain though? Can you just have such a strong will to die that you just stop living?"

That is when I heard it; the words still echo in my head, loud and clear. "There comes a time in your life when you come to the realization that you are more desperate than embarrassed, and that is when you seek help." I stared at the speaker. Did he just say that? I wanted to cry. I was so incredibly embarrassed that I could not stand for anyone to pity me. I had been judged before. Pity made me sick to my stomach. "Oh, you poor thing." Translation: "I feel for you, you whore." Desperate was an understatement though. I had been sitting there thinking about suicide for the past hour, and it was not the first time.

I hardly remember what happened next. I know I grabbed you, whom I had hardly talked to before, and took you outside. I told you everything; every stupid, minuscule mistake I had made. I did not leave out a single detail. For the first time in my life, I was not judged for what I had done. You were so kind and actually showed me love! How could someone be so kind?

I learned that God could replace that emptiness in my heart. He did not promise it would be easy but that I would always be loved no matter what. All I had to do was trust. I learned that He would make something beautiful out of my pain and struggles. All that was lost could be found in Him.

That summer, I learned that God makes all things new. All my pain, all that was lost, my screwed-up life, He would chisel at me. It might hurt, but He would make me into a new and beautiful thing.

This was not as easy as one conversation, and all the internal struggle ceased. No, the choice to live is a decision that many of us make every day, and it is not always an easy one. Some days you may want to argue that choosing life is not a viable option, that the struggles associated with your mental health or physical diagnosis are too great. The thing I have come to see, though, is that as long as I draw breath, there is a purpose for my life. And even if it is not known to me, the day that I choose to take my life, I choose to abandon God's call on my life. As long as I draw breath, He can and He will use me. I choose to live so my death will not be in vain.

Choose life too.

September 8, 2024

Today I am struggling
I saw you
I saw it in your eyes
I have felt that before

A shame that
Weighs you down
Walls you off from people
For fear of their reaction

It takes from you
Your whole personality
Your whole being
It chips away

God, use me
If I can do or say
Something—anything
To bring glory to You

Make the opportunity available
Use me
Use me
Use me

October 6, 2024

Hear me now
This will pass
You will grow and thrive
I know this

I know because
I've been there
Caged and then set free
God did that

Not me
I can do nothing
Nothing by my own power
God can

Let Him use you
Moving forward
Be His voice and let Him use you
Be the example

Your past
It's not a hindrance
It is a tool God can use
For His glory alone

My Reflection

God has a purpose for each of us. Righteous is He and His ways. I could never understand His plan; everything is intentional and to bring Him glory. He is the beginning and the end.

And yet here is the hardest thing to pray: "In all things may Your will be done."

October 6, 2024

It's hard to remember that I, in fact, have a purpose.

Just a few years ago, I had all but forgotten.

Sometimes things are going so well that I forget to praise God. Instead, I say with boastful pride in my heart, "Look what I have done; look what I have accomplished; look how good I am." And then comes the snare: "Would you ever ___________?" Never! And I am drawn into a sin I was not guarding against. Because "look what I have done; look what I have accomplished; look how good I am."

The blank is left on purpose because we can fill it with so many things. I filled that blank, and I filled my heart and mind with things that should not have had a place in my life. I sat on the stairs and stared at a bottle filled with something else entirely. Now my pride is wounded, and in my heart and mind I hear, "Look what I have done. Look how I have failed. Look how terrible I am." And this bottle of pills promises to take it all away.

No! God, break me free of those chains! Free me from the cage I create for myself over and over again.

October 6, 2017

I am a passionate person
Once, early in my relationship with my husband
I was speaking to my mom
Speaking about the illnesses that plague him
It is easy to talk to her about these things
Since she lost my dad early in their marriage
She said that the two of us are passionate people
We love deeply,
And I will love him with a fierce,
Deep love for as long as I have him,
Just as she did with my dad
I feel deeply for people
I cry in movies
I cry when people I know feel loss
I rejoice when the people I know are happy
I share in all their emotions, good and bad
I could not choose a life where I did not help people

October 2, 2024

Isn't life funny?
Those full-circle moments that come into our lives
Being reminded of my dreams
My goals and plans
I journaled in my twenties
My written desires are so strong to make a difference
Adamant that I could not choose that kind of life
The kind where I did not help people
I did not know how
I did not know when
I did not know where
And then, for some reason
I found myself with two degrees
unsure exactly how I would use them
Yet I found my place
And now I write to you,
You will find your place too

My Reflection

It's one thing to look back at ten years of journal entries or more and say, "Now look how that worked out." It's so hard in the day-to-day to see how one action could make such a difference. I think the most excellent piece of advice my mom ever gave me was this: "Don't do anything on Saturday that will keep you from church on Sunday." However, she meant it very literally. I've kept it in my heart and on my mind because while I agree, I think it applies to all things. Do not let your actions today, which will bring short-term satisfaction, affect your goals or what is important to you for your future.

I hope you hold onto your dreams, too, because with time and perseverance, you will find your place as well. Every small action counts toward the greater picture of your life, and I can tell you that life will get hard, and it can be disheartening when you try and try, only to feel like nothing is coming together. But in those moments, it's essential to remember that perseverance is key. Just because immediate results aren't visible doesn't diminish the value of your efforts.

October 11, 2024

I am here
I put in effort
But nothing came to me
Except maybe discouragement
But why?
I still showed up
I still tried

My Reflection

Are you still with me? I know this ride has a lot of ups and downs. I told you this was for the people like me who ride the waves of emotions. I've also told you the choice to live is a choice so many of us choose every day. Some days you just have to wake up and get up. Even when you cannot see it, you still have a purpose as long as you draw breath.

August 25, 2025

She asked if I missed my calling
What an odd thing to say
Hot wind from the outside blows in
My skin prickles
My career and success seem so obvious
But then to hear this
This nudge toward a westward path
I glance over my shoulder
Then push forward to the north
What propels me to stay my course?
I cannot name it

Sometime in September 2024

Boats in the desert
I pass one after another
I laugh at them
Their perceived lack of purpose
Until the realization hits me
My view is limited
They have a purpose
They are here for a reason
One I cannot see
One I cannot understand
It's like all of us
Some days I am a boat in the desert
I still have a purpose

June 9, 2025

I've had numerous conversations lately with friends and colleagues about the perceived loss of or lack of purpose. The same thought comes to mind: "Friend, if you draw breath, you have purpose!"

Do we all struggle? Do we all at some point or another feel the emptiness of our day? Every day we draw breath is such a gift, and your purpose for the day—when you see no other reason for moving forward—can be found in building up those around you.

Sometime in March 2023

You have been on a plateau for a while now
Wanting desperately to be of use
. . . but not
Because to be of use requires surrender

January 4, 2011

Throughout life, we face hard times
Many people say these trials make us stronger
I believe they make us
No stronger
And no weaker
They simply shape us
Into who we will be
In the end
How strong or weak
Depends on one thing
How much of our lives do we put in God's hands?

My Reflection

And still, the hardest prayer to whisper is this: "Let Your will be done in all things."

Chapter 2

Time

October 19, 2021

Time.

It is precious, so I will try to be brief. It has been on my mind a lot this month with another birthday approaching. I am now two years away from thirty. Go on, roll your eyes. Everyone does. Even my own mother teases, though I don't know how she could forget that my dad's thirtieth birthday was his last. People say, "You have time," but did he? I think he did, but if I died, would I have had enough?

Time is precious no matter if you are seven or seventy, and what you do with it matters. This time we are in is different for each of us. It may be a time of relief for some or a time of chaos for others. In times like these, I find myself in Ecclesiastes 3 where we get a long list of "there is a time for this, and there is a time for that."

It matters less what I have done with my life and more that I have let God use me to my fullest potential . . .

at all times . . .
in all seasons.

My Reflection

As I transition my thoughts from purpose to time, the concepts start to intertwine. I think it is possible to consider purpose from a position of detachment; yet when time is considered, a sense of urgency takes over.

I heard this recording of Billy Graham once that said, "Indecision in itself is a choice. not to decide is to decide not to. . . . Decisions are made whether we make them or not. Time decides if you will not and time always decides against you."[1]

God's timing is perfect, but we have the autonomy to choose to live life with purpose for His glory or to squander opportunity.

---

[1] Billy Graham Evangelistic Association, *Billy Graham – Timeless Truth – Change,* YouTube video, December 5, 2008, 3:19, https://www.youtube.com/watch?v=inLmaG6qR7E

October 13 2024

Have you ever said
"What a coincidence"?
Typically, it's over something simple
We laugh—we giggle—we tease
But then we encounter a "coincidence"
And it alters a potential outcome for the better
How can we still believe it is by chance?
I do not believe it is
No, no, I believe it is God working in your life
That is divine timing

My Reflection

Despite my awareness of the precious nature of time, I occasionally find myself losing track of it. I flow with the tides, motions mapped out and predictable. My actions are like a choreographed dance that repetition has made me capable of performing with no thought. When the realization of how much time has passed confronts me, I am left in shock.

November 3, 2024

"Hey, how are you? I haven't seen you in a while."

I hate that phrase. I hear it too much. I don't like being reminded that I've been in another one of those phases, and being aware doesn't make it easier to get out. It pushes me farther back.

I don't have an answer for you if you experience this, and I don't have a solution for myself either.

November 1, 2011

Sometimes I wonder about how much energy and time

How much effort I put into things

How many things do I attempt to make work

That were never meant to be attempted in the first place

My Reflection

When time gets away from me, it seems like I have been operating with blinders on. I saw something, someone, some concept, and it became my heart's desire. I've become like a horse in a race, saddled by the driving force of desire. Blinders are on, and I am sightless to all but the path to my goal. However, once I reach the line, the victory is short-lived. There is no lasting impact.

Frustration mounts. Yes, I have reached my goal; I have spent a great deal of time and energy in attaining it. But what am I left with?

March 25, 2025

2:20 a.m.
My eyes open, and I am wide awake
Fear grips me, panic slowly takes hold

2:45 a.m.
The ceiling looks the same
I can find no answers there

3:15 a.m.
The lights of the gym look like a promise
An exhaustion is ahead that will quiet my mind

4:10 a.m.
Praise the Lord for the quiet that penetrates my mind
Praise the Lord for outlets for the emotions that paralyze

August 25, 2025

I gave my life to a cause
I thought it was noble
I thought I was right
I gave and I gave
I fought for what was right
The fallout was ugly
The years that I spent were tainted
Was it actually noble?
Was it actually right?
Maybe, probably
But what is left?
The memories are bitter
Ties ripped to shreds
So much confusion
So many questions
I suppose I will just move forward
I cannot find the purpose in looking back

September 30, 2024

Roz,
Today is hard—I feel your loss acutely
Last night I dreamed I saw you, and we talked
Today I was reminded that I will never again
Have your guidance or your wisdom
My pride wasted the time I had left with you

January 16, 2014

Dad,

I still remember visiting the church where you worked.

I remember sitting on the steps in front of the pulpit in the sanctuary.

I remember singing those praise songs from the transparencies and being perfectly content.

When I close my eyes

I can see the dark sanctuary dimly lit by the light flowing in from the stained-glass windows.

I can feel the rough, primary-green carpet under my fingers.

I can smell the strong scent of lemon-lime Lysol,

Which must have been used in great abundance.

But

I cannot hear the sweet sound of your voice.

June 11, 2025

Roz,

Grief sucks.

I was on my way to work today when the sight of a garden caught my eye.

Your loss came forth in a tidal wave that poured over my cheeks and soaked my collar.

I had a vision of you in heaven, tending to your vegetables, laughing with your momma by your side.

I know you missed her, but now I miss you.

Grief sucks.

August 25, 2025

Roz,

I miss you.

I've spent a significant amount of time wondering what you would say to my current struggles.

I miss sitting in your office, eager for your wisdom in every situation.

I know you would not say "I told you so," but you did tell me so.

My pride said stay when your wisdom said go.

That's hindsight.

Sometime in September 2024

Someone died today
You were mad because you were behind schedule
But someone died today
You were mad because traffic was slow
But someone died today
You said, "There better be a good reason for this."
And then you saw the lights, the debris, the crushed truck
Someone died today

September 24, 2024

Roz,
Today I learned you died
I was sitting at a bagel shop in another state
They didn't want to tell me you died
Not while I was away
I found out through a slip-up
The grief comes in waves
I think it's strange
You don't realize how deep the roots go
The roots of your relationship
Until it is plucked away by death
And you are confronted with grief
Thank you for all the lessons you taught me
Your legacy lives on
I love you

Undated

For some time I have carried this mantra: Today I will do my best, and though my best today may not look like yesterday's or tomorrow's, it will still be 100 percent of what I have today, and that's okay.

For even in my relationships, I will not split the effort 50/50. I will give 100 percent of what I have every day. I will not hold back a portion of my energy and say, "Well, here you go . . . this is 50 percent of what I have today. What have you brought?"

No, I will humbly lay down all that is within me for the love of my God, for the love of my husband and family, and for the love of my community.

Sometime in September 2024

As I get ready to leave work after another long day, I think about my coworker's words as he, the last in the building other than me, said, "You are doing great, but don't forget you have to live life."

But is this not life? Is this not my legacy I am building? What will it say? "She got to go home and watch a show every night"?

Or will my efforts have a greater impact, my name just a whisper in the wind, a name forgotten but a foundation laid for the next generation to build on?

January 13, 2024

Wait!
Can you not just be patient?
Just for a moment
This back and forth that you do
You have me on edge
Pause
Breathe
We do not have to do this right now

Chapter 3

Struggle

October 2, 2024

She doesn't want to hear problems
Not without a ready solution
I grab hold of the problem
I fight it with prayer

God is my salvation
He is my protection

My Reflection

Struggle carries too much negative connotation for something so constant in life. We struggle against time. We struggle to find our purpose. We struggle to press through grief. Recently, I struggled to stay awake at work. Today, I struggle to find the words to convey to you what I feel in my heart. Struggle is the forge we use to fire a masterpiece. And in this chapter, when you see the word *struggle* or perceive the struggle below the surface of my words, I want you to envision a forge . . .

And perhaps you will catch a glimpse of what is in the fire.

September 30, 2024

It is an odd thing to realize that your struggles also belonged to those who came before you—to realize that while you may feel like a fraud, an imposter, forced to live up to some standard you cannot attain, you were never alone.

> *My prayer to God today is a sincere plea for forgiveness from the selfish nature in me that I've allowed to surface. My prayer is that God will continue to use me in spite of that. I know that in order to continue leading in the ministry, I must keep myself as clean as possible (with His help of course). But even with God's help, we still get to choose to sin or accept the victory He has won for us over that sin. . . . I know that if I commit my works to you, Lord, you will establish my thoughts, and I know that with every task, You will be there to help me through.*
>
> *—Steve Moore, April 15, 1996*

You may have fought selfishness, or you may be fighting pride. Maybe you feel lazy or lustful, greedy or gluttonous.

I have struggled with many things, but I am not the first, and you will not be the last.

DON'T YOU KNOW THAT THE RUNNERS IN A STADIUM ALL RACE, BUT ONLY ONE RECEIVES THE PRIZE? RUN IN SUCH A WAY TO WIN THE PRIZE. NOW EVERYONE WHO COMPETES EXERCISES SELF-CONTROL IN EVERYTHING. HOWEVER, THEY DO IT TO RECEIVE A CROWN THAT WILL FADE AWAY, BUT WE A CROWN THAT WILL NEVER FADE AWAY. THEREFORE I DO NOT RUN LIKE ONE WHO RUNS AIMLESSLY OR BOX LIKE ONE BEATING THE AIR. INSTEAD, I DISCIPLINE MY BODY AND BRING IT UNDER STRICT CONTROL, SO THAT AFTER PREACHING TO OTHERS, I MYSELF WILL NOT BE DISQUALIFIED.

—I COR. 9:24–27 HCSB

November 12, 2015

Hey, I saw your post from last night.
I know in reality I don't really know you,
And you don't really know me,
But I couldn't not say anything.
For a period of time
I wasn't who everyone expected me to be.
This idea of who they thought I was,
It was enough to make me want to be dead
A whole lot more than living.
In my mind, I wouldn't have the guilt anymore.
One night I was listening to this man.
He said there comes a time when you are more desperate for a change
Than embarrassed about what's going on, and that's when you get help.
From that day, I have learned a few things.
I'm going to make mistakes,
But . . . God is bigger.
My mistakes are not too much for Him.
My mistakes could never screw up God's plans
No matter what.
He will not leave me nor forsake me (Deut. 31:6).

My Reflection

He will always be the lamp unto my feet and the light upon my path (Ps. 119:105),

But He won't force me to follow.

HE NEVER GROWS FAINT OR WEARY; THERE IS NO LIMIT TO HIS UNDERSTANDING. HE GIVES STRENGTH TO THE WEARY AND STRENGTHENS THE POWERLESS. YOUTHS MAY FAINT AND GROW WEARY, AND YOUNG MEN STUMBLE AND FALL, BUT THOSE WHO TRUST IN THE LORD WILL RENEW THEIR STRENGTH; THEY WILL SOAR ON WINGS LIKE EAGLES; THEY WILL RUN AND NOT GROW WEARY; THEY WILL WALK AND NOT FAINT.

—ISA. 40:28–31 HCSB

October 4, 2024

Choose to love the people around you with such a love that you would gladly give your life for theirs, but you would never take your life and leave them without you.

The world is never better without you in it.

November 10, 2024

Sometimes I wonder why it feels like I'm the only one who really struggles with a wandering mind. I know what I want and who I want to be, but the same desires keep resurfacing. How can we want two things at the same time that are so contradictory?

December 25, 2024

I want
I desire
I crave
My mouth waters with need
And yet satisfaction never comes
I get what I seek
Yet something hollow follows
More
More
More
Nothing
I pause, I pivot, and I see another object I desire
I repeat
Again . . . I am unsatisfied
So I repeat

December 31, 2024

The night was dark
So is the morning
I tried to feel
It was empty
The lack of everything
It was suffocating
I cannot feel the air
Is it there?
I cannot breathe
I don't really want to

January 22, 2025

I had to let go of what I treasured in order to do what was necessary. What I found so precious weighed me down; it was a chest of gold chained to my feet at the bottom of raging waters. I thought it was grounding me, yet when I finally broke my chains, I was able to surface the water. It was the change in perspective, the breath of oxygen it provided me, and the strength I needed to go back and save what was important.

February 5, 1997

From the journal of Steve Moore:

My emotions are remaining on a roller coaster that will not end. At one time, I can see a year from now, everything remaining as if it had never happened. Having a wonderful testimony to share with everyone I come in contact with. At other times, I can see the Lord bringing me home. This is a roller coaster in itself. I'm so ready to go home (heaven) I can taste it. But I struggle because I want to stay down here with my beautiful wife and darling child. Paul had the same struggle. He said so in Philippians.

June 9, 2025

Constant movement—tired but somewhat fulfilled.

"Too social."

Solution: reduce and add productivity.

Overwhelming list—unexplained sadness.

"I've missed you."

Solution: People need people; get out more.

Up seven pounds—so bloated and uncomfortable.

"What are you going to do about it?"

Solution: 4:00 a.m. alarm; title: Gym.

Deadlines—panic and forgetfulness for companions.

"You're doing too much."

. . .

Repeat.

Chapter 4
Gratitude

October 13, 2024

A night of gratitude,
Praise to my God in heaven!
I have so many things to thank You for.
Thank You for making the way for me to process my feelings.
Thank You for the people around me who will come alongside me and pray with me.
Thank You for giving me the people I love: community.
Thank You for Your continued guidance.
Thank You for holding me close.
Thank You for the continued opportunity to share You and what You have done for me.
Thank You for helping me surrender my pride.
Thank You for the time I have with the ones I love.
Thank You for friendships.

My Reflection

Why is it so difficult to ponder what is good in life when what is negative is dwelt on so easily? I can make you feel my pain, my emotion, and my strife with a few words. Yet when I sit down with intention to rejoice with you in what is good, I cannot easily find the words to convey it to you.

June 9, 2025

I've been thinking about the workings of our minds
Or at least the workings of my own
I saw the word "thankfulness."
I opened my book to write what I was sure would be profound

The eloquence of writing is lost to me
What comes is a gentle reminder
I have not dwelt on God's blessings as of late
And I am so thankful for a new day to begin again

October 2, 2024

My husband is my absolute best friend.
The two of us love to be together.
On the road trip the two of us just took
We spent every second together.
As I sit and think about life so far,
I am overwhelmed with gratitude.
He is the love of my life
Probably too often I say,
"Hey, you know what?"
"What?"
"I Love You!"
There is no room in my heart for regret.

My Reflection

Is this the end of this chapter? Is this all there is to be thankful for? It is quite horrifying that this is all I have for you. I've never had the need to sit down and write about the things I am thankful for. I believe it's largely due to having no shortage of people who want to visit with us about the good in our life. We have a whole holiday dedicated to Thanksgiving.

But this book is not just for the happy things, but the other stuff too—the mess and the junk we don't want others to see. Remember, I don't mean to give guidance; I would like to just be honest. Frankly, this is what life looks like: a big jumble of every kind of emotion. Some come in greater frequency than others, but their value and importance are not diminished by that.

Chapter 5

Love

But what about love?

We justify so many things in its name. Some great acts go down in history, and some are far more infamous. The desire for love and the lack thereof has been a sign erected on the road of life that has quite a track record for sending people, including myself, off track if it's not interpreted properly.

January 16, 2014

I have come to the realization that there is a great longing somewhere in the deepest part of my being to be told I am loved. When I am told I am loved, it is like a tiny ember breaks through the ashes of a long burnt-out fire—a fire that was once kindled with three powerful words, day in and day out, so very many years ago: "I love you." With my dad, it seemed love was in every conversation and every goodbye. Anytime the three of us had to part, we would hold up a hand with thumb, pointer finger, and pinkie extended, middle and ring fingers pressed down—the sign for I love you.

To taste such love—a love born of not only being someone's child, which many have not felt, but the love of a man who loved all people so deeply regardless of their choices or struggles. Love came easily to him because of the love he had been shown that he accepted and reflected so completely.

September 30, 2024

In this world, love gets so twisted. I would actually go as far as to say, the idea of love gets twisted. We think we know love, but we do not. We create for ourselves an image of love, but it is our own image and ideas we build it from. How can we then expect it to be perfect when we ourselves are flawed?

October 6, 2024

I remember my search to grasp love
I remember because some days
I'm still searching
Not because I do not have it
But because I lived so long searching
So very long looking for my interpretation of it
So long, in fact, that sometimes I forget . . .
That's not love
I thought love was being enough for a person, enough that they, in turn, were enough for you,

Or maybe it was giving away your beating heart, hoping it was enough for the next person,

Or the next.

The quest for love was one of searching out a love I could be enough to earn . . .

enough

to

earn
If you have ever tried to earn love, how did that turn out?

What a disappointment that has turned out for me.

October 9, 2013

I am approaching rock bottom
My phone doesn't ring anymore
The guys, they don't reply
It won't take long now
For depression to take hold
So completely like before
Soon all my adventures
They will feel more like a daydream
Less than a memory
because there will be no one
No one to ruminate over them with me
Its twenty days 'til my birthday
Will anyone even remember?
Probably not

My Reflection

The audacity of my heart to turn away from what I had been taught and what I had been so graciously bestowed! The audacity of my treacherous mind to abandon the wisdom of the God I claimed to know and the elders who had gone before me!

September 29, 2024

In life so far I have learned a few things
And the greatest of these is this
When your hope is in people
They will fail you
BUT God . . .
He will never forget you.

HE NEVER GROWS FAINT OR WEARY; THERE IS NO LIMIT TO HIS UNDERSTANDING. HE GIVES STRENGTH TO THE WEARY AND STRENGTHENS THE POWERLESS. YOUTHS MAY FAINT AND GROW WEARY, AND YOUNG MEN STUMBLE AND FALL, BUT THOSE WHO TRUST IN THE LORD WILL RENEW THEIR STRENGTH; THEY WILL SOAR ON WINGS LIKE EAGLES; THEY WILL RUN AND NOT GROW WEARY; THEY WILL WALK AND NOT FAINT.

—ISA. 40:28–31 HCSB

My Reflection

The wisdom of God is far greater than my mind could fathom, his love far more than my heart could ever hold. God's love is what enabled my father to love without condition.

My faith is in knowing that my Heavenly Father must really love me a lot or He wouldn't have died in my place on that cross, and if He loves me that much, He has my best interest in mind.

—Steve Moore, February 2, 1997
six days before his twenty-seventh
birthday in the midst of
his battle with cancer

January 16, 2014

My father was my absolute best friend
The two of us loved to be together
In the videos the two of us made
We would just talk
As I sit and watch what is left of the videos
I am overwhelmed with grief
He would say, "I love you"
Over and over
"Do you know how much I love you?"
"Do you love me too?"
I seldom replied
It fills my heart with regret

It was Christmas 1999

Dad had been sick for almost three years. His time was coming fast.

He had already lived so much longer than the doctors anticipated, but very soon his condition would rapidly deteriorate.

This Christmas, however, my father gave me the most beautiful and wonderful gift that would later become my most prized possession.

To anyone else it would be just a charm, a piece of jewelry of too high a price to give a six-year-old, but the small, silver charm was so much more.

There were two charms on beautiful silver chains, one for me and one for my mom.

The charm was a silver, three-dimensional hand with the thumb, pointer finger, and pinkie extended, the middle and ring fingers pressed down and the James Avery symbol carved into the back.

The charm meant "I love you." He would die three months later.

Those three months would be the hardest. He would forget words that were lost from his memory altogether.

Hospice came in one day, and my parent's room was turned into a hospital room.

He would lose his motor skills and then become paralyzed.

He would lose his sight and his speech.

They said all he could do in the end was hear.

I remember once in those three months sitting on the hospital bed staring at him and just taking it all in.

I told him I loved him, but he said nothing back. He could not speak.

The man who had once told me every second of every day that he loved me so very much now had no words.

My mom took his hand and raised his thumb, pointer finger, and pinkie and pressed down his middle and ring fingers.

She put my hand on his and said, "Look, he loves you too."

I knew what she had done. "No, Momma, you made him do that."

Without hesitation she responded, "But I know what Daddy wants to say to you, and he wants to tell you he loves you too."

That is the last memory I have of him before the night of his death.

Years later I got the notion that my father must have left some secret note for me to find when I was older.

It could have been from watching one too many movies, but there had to be something left just for me.

I searched for years with no success and was incredibly discouraged until one day something in the mirror caught my eye.

I looked down at my necklace that I had worn for so many years, only removed from my neck if it was absolutely necessary, which was very rare.

All this time I had been looking for some note hidden away in a dusty box or old Bible that told me how much he loved me one more time.

All along, I had worn a secret message of my very own from him around my neck that told me every day "I love you" over and over again, just like he did when I was little.

Chapter 6

Growth

January 22, 2025

Is all growth visual?
If growth has a sound
How can I learn to hear its sweet subtle voice
To appreciate growth's work in progress
There is something so profound in the process of change
To experience it in the moment
Rather than merely viewing the end result

Sometime in September 2024

There is something in the wind
I take a deep breath
And smell life
Change
Growth

My Reflection

This is the end, but it's not the end. It's just life so far. I've grown significantly through this process. I have developed as a person and have been given the gift of understanding in some areas. I have learned a little bit about myself as I have read my struggles from the past and seen my growth through it. I have moved past the little girl who would scribble in journals until she ran out of ink and then burn the pages so no one would see them.

I'm still learning and still growing. I am still processing some things, some feelings. It turns out that there were some life lessons I wasn't ready to share.

I think a long chapter on growth would be profound. I could not think of a better way to conclude than to show growth in leaps and bounds—or even a slow trickle of growth over time in countless small entries.

Upon reflection, though, I am happy with the growth displayed from beginning to end. I've learned that growth is subtle, and I can see it in the struggle and in my purpose. So this is Life So Far. Maybe one day I will share a little more life with you.

About the Author

Lindsey Christian is an author and accountant from East Texas, where she lives with her husband of eight years, Alan. She discovered writing at a young age, turning to journaling as a safe place to express her grief and emotions when words were too heavy to speak aloud.

Years later, after the loss of a treasured mentor in her early thirties, Lindsey's private reflections took a new path. Alan read her journal entries and gently encouraged her to share her voice with others — a turning point that led her to pursue writing beyond the page of her notebook.

When she isn't writing, Lindsey works at the intersection of finance and healthcare — a calling that, much like her storytelling, is driven by service, compassion, and community.

www.ingramcontent.com/pod-product-compliance
Lightning Source LLC
LaVergne TN
LVHW010628100826
845148LV00014B/3162

* 9 7 8 1 6 8 4 8 8 1 6 3 5 *